D0385117

God is Good!

Given to _____

On this _____ day of _____

By _____

With this special message . . .

_____

_____

_____

God is Good!

Inspiration from
Robert H. Schuller

THOMAS NELSON
PUBLISHERS

Copyright © 1993 by
Thomas Nelson Publishers

Published in Nashville, Tennessee by
Thomas Nelson Publishers.

**Library of Congress
Cataloging-in-Publication Data**

Schuller, Robert Harold.
    God is Good / Robert H. Schuller.
        p.   cm. — (Itty Bitty book)
    ISBN 0-8407-6308-5 (TR)
    ISBN 0-7852-8265-3 (MM)
    1. Christian life—1960—Quotations,
maxims, etc. 2. Self-actualization
(Psychology)—Religious aspects—
Quotations, maxims, etc.
I. Title II. Series.
BV4905.2.S37   1993
242—dc20   93–12208
                                    CIP

Printed in Hong Kong
1 2 3 4 5 6 7 — 98 97 96 95 94 93

God is Good!

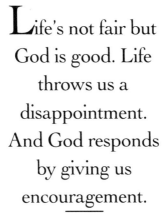

Life's not fair but
God is good. Life
throws us a
disappointment.
And God responds
by giving us
encouragement.

KNOW THAT TIME PERFORMS MIRACLES.

When something
seems impossible,
leave the door open to
this idea . . . It just
might be possible.

PROBLEMS ARE GUIDELINES, NOT STOP SIGNS.

It's better to do something imperfectly, than to do nothing perfectly.

IF YOU CAN DREAM IT, YOU CAN DO IT!

Every time one door

closes . . . another

one opens!

LOOK FOR THE GOOD AND YOU WILL FIND IT.

A prescription for joyful living: "Be good, be kind, be unselfish."

Every Problem Can Be a Possibility in Disguise.

Happiness is
a readjusted
mental attitude.

BELIEVE IN THE GOD WHO BELIEVES IN YOU.

If you listen to
your fears you will
die never knowing
what a great person
you might
have been.

SELECT SELF-RESPECT . . . NOT SELF-PITY.

See and seize the possibilities within yourself.

MAKE YOUR SUFFERING A PASSAGE, NOT A DEAD END.

Real love
releases hidden
possibilities.

PLANT POSITIVE THOUGHTS AND EXPECT A HARVEST OF GREAT POSSIBILITIES.

———

Self-confidence

cannot be taught . . . it

must be caught.

THE TASSEL IS WORTH THE HASSLE.
GRADUATION.

There is almost no problem that patience cannot solve . . . and no dream it cannot push to victory.

EVERY ADVERSITY
HIDES A POSSIBILITY.

When you're good . . . you're good . . . when you're not . . . you're human.

Invest in today, for even the setting of the sun is not a day's finale, but every day gains a piece of eternity when it is woven into history.

DARING TO DREAM IS DARING TO LIVE!

GOD USES LIFE'S BRUISES.

God does not promise skies always blue ... but ... He does promise to see us through.

A GIVING ATTITUDE IS THE SECRET TO SUCCESSFUL LIVING.

Happiness is . . .
having a hand to
hold . . . finding a
heart to heal . . . and
leaning into
tomorrow with love.

GRACE IS GOD'S LOVE IN ACTION FOR THOSE WHO DON'T DESERVE IT.

Bad times become
good times when
they bring out the
best in you.

You can draw great dividends from your deepest difficulties.

Selfishness turns
life into burdens,
while selflessness
turns burdens into
life.

Happy Is the Heart Who Offers the Lonely a Friend.

No matter how
obstinate the obstacle
or horrific the hurt,
forgiveness is ALWAYS
possible.

The deepest need
of the human being
is the need to be
needed—so—make
it a point to meet
someone's need
today.

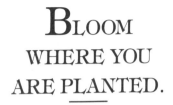

BLOOM
WHERE YOU
ARE PLANTED.

JUST AS YOU
BELIEVE IN SEAS
YOU'VE NEVER
SAILED, SO BELIEVE
IN A LOVE YOU'VE
NEVER FELT FROM
THE GOD YOU'VE
NEVER SEEN.

Love is . . . deciding
to make your problem
my <u>problem</u>.

LOVE
WITHOUT
FAITH IS
IMPOSSIBLE —
AND — FAITH
WITHOUT
LOVE IS
UNACCEPTABLE.

Perfect love
perceives people not
as problems, but as
possibilities.

Be Happy!
You Are
Loved.

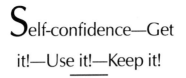

Self-confidence—Get it!—Use it!—Keep it!

Mind clearing produces power steering. When your mind is clear, you will have the power to steer your life without any difficulty!

YOU CAN BECOME THE PERSON YOU WANT TO BE!

If you want to live,
you have to give.
This is the key to
prosperity. This is
also the key to
joyful living.

LIFE IS WORTH LIVING WHEN YOU FIND A GOD THAT'S WORTH SERVING.

HOPE IS AN IMPORTANT HUMAN VALUE FOR DYNAMIC LIVING. WHERE THERE IS HOPE, THERE IS LIFE!

There is only one
way to conquer fear
and that is to face it!
Come-alive-power
gives courage!

TOTAL PEACE WILL ONLY COME FROM TOTAL COMMITMENT.

WHEN IT RAINS, LOOK FOR THE RAINBOW.

The exciting path
is the narrow road
that winds through
the mountains. It's
the narrow path
through the garden
that leads to the
secluded little spots.

I don't believe there is a value that is more recognizable and admirable in a human life than courage. God wants you to be courageous!

To endure means:
"Inch by inch,
anything's a cinch."

How Do You Move a Mountain? You Move a Mountain One Truckload at a Time. You Chisel Away One Chip at a Time.

LIFE IS GROWTH.

TIME WAITS FOR
NO ONE. GIVE
YOUR GOAL AND
DREAM ALL YOU'VE
GOT! LET GO—AND
LET GOD MAKE
IT HAPPEN IN
HIS WAY.

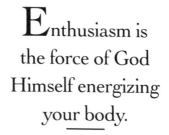

Enthusiasm is
the force of God
Himself energizing
your body.

If you don't believe
in yourself, who will?
You owe yourself
every possible
chance!

IF YOU DON'T HAVE A VISION FOR YOUR LIFE, THEN YOU PROBABLY HAVEN'T FOCUSED IN ON ANYTHING.

Try to turn enemies into friends. People who belittle people, will be little people—and accomplish little.

EVERY PROBLEM IS
TEMPORARY. EVERY
VALLEY HAS ITS
LOW POINT. REACH
IT AND THERE'S
ONLY ONE WAY TO
GO FROM THAT
POINT, AND THAT'S
UPWARD.

Look at your imperfections and respect yourself anyway.

WHEN LIFE HANDS YOU A BIG DISAPPOINTMENT, IT'S TIME TO MAKE NEW PLANS. IT'S

TIME TO GET A
POSITIVE PLAN
ON HOW YOU
ARE GOING TO
HANDLE THIS
DISAPPOINTMENT.

Be thankful for all the storms of your life that have blown out, blown over, or passed you by and never touched you.

God Promises Mercy Adequate Enough to Meet Any Tragedy.

Nobody can do it alone. We all need the loving support of family or a caring friend.

It takes courage to love. It takes a brave heart that risks being broken to discover the joy of <u>love</u>.

ARE YOU LIVING RIGHT?
WHEN YOU LIVE RIGHT, YOU WON'T BE DISAPPOINTED. YOU'LL BE

ABLE TO LOOK
IN THE
MIRROR AND
BE PROUD OF
THE PERSON
YOU ARE.

Build bridges of

love.

We Discover
True Friendship
When False Ones
Forsake Us. We
Learn to Prize
Freedom When We
Are in Danger of
Losing It.

WHEN LIFE'S
NOT FAIR, THE
FIRST THING
TO REMEMBER
IS TO BE
CAREFUL. BE
CAREFUL HOW
YOU REACT
AND WHAT

HAPPENS TO
YOU. BE FAIR
TO YOURSELF.
CHOOSE TO
REACT
POSITIVELY,
NOT
NEGATIVELY.

We learn
courage when we
face danger, we
learn patience when
we endure suffering,
we learn tenderness
when we taste pain.

If you want to live positively, you start by learning to love positively.

Today Is a New
Day. You Are
Worthy of a New
Dream. You Are
God's Dream and
"God Don't Make
No Junk!"

God believes in you and He can't be <u>wrong</u>!

Y OU CAN HANDLE DISAPPOINTMENT AS LONG AS YOU ARE PROUD OF WHO

YOU ARE. LIVE
IN SUCH A WAY
THAT YOU
WON'T BE
ASHAMED OF
WHAT YOU DO.

WHEN YOU
CAN'T SEE THE
GOODNESS, WHEN
THE HURT IS TOO
GREAT, THEN START
WITH FORGIVENESS.
THAT WILL LEAD
YOU TO SEE THE
GOODNESS.

Good can do
tremendous things
through the person
who doesn't care who
gets the credit.
———

I CAN LIVE
WITHOUT
PLEASURE,
BUT I CAN'T
LIVE IN
SHAME.
PEOPLE
CANNOT

HUMILIATE
ME, THEY
CANNOT STRIP
ME OF MY
PRIDE. I HAVE
A LIFE AND I
AM PROUD OF
WHO I AM.

Birds Were
Meant to Fly.
Flowers Were
Meant to Bloom.
Humans Were
Designed to
Believe: in Beauty,
in Love, in Truth,
in God. . .

The most important thing is living your life for something more important than your life.